Make-Ahead Mix Day

Make-Ahead Mix Day

Complete Recipes and Instructions for On-Hand Homemade Quick Mixes

Mary Ellen Ward

www.thehomemadehomestead.com

To my up-and-coming Baking Queen and insatiable bibliophile, I dedicate this first book to my much-loved daughter, Josselyn.

…How about a good book and a brownie?

To state it very simply,

Make Ahead Mix Day is an outline of all you need to prepare a pantry full of baking mixes to have on hand regularly and reliably, laid out in an easy-read, easy-to-use format.

This quick reference was designed to help you speed through the task of stocking up your pantry with wholesome fare; fare in which you maintain total control over the type and quality of the ingredients that you use, and which minimizes your family's exposure to unnecessary chemicals and preservatives.

Table of Contents

The Make-Ahead Mix Day Concept

Make Ahead Mix Day grew simply enough out of a regular practice here in my home. It was motivated primarily by two factors: first, the desire to regularly provide more healthful, wholesome foods and baked goods, minus all the preservatives and unknown chemicals abundant in store-shelf foods; and second, the need and desire to cut down our household grocery budget to a manageable level while also continuing to eat well and have foods we enjoy.

As a family of six this is something of a challenge, particularly when you start considering the harried, busy nature of life in these modern times. Even for a primarily homesteading family like mine, limiting extraneous and extra-curricular activities as we are, getting mostly homemade goods that I know and trust into everyone's belly, lunch box, and snack plate every day is a challenge. As much as I like to think that I can forgo all the modern conveniences and just whip up a made-from-scratch treat instead, the reality is that life is BUSY. There always seems to be just one (or twenty) things too many to do, and time is always of the essence.

This left me in a sort of limbo because I really wanted to get back to my "from scratch" roots (I can still recall the disdain of my childhood when *gasp* someone made a birthday cake from a box mix of all things!). I wanted to return to those roots because in all honesty what we ate when I was young was just plain better. Growing up on a New England dairy farm we didn't eat a lot of boxed or pre-packaged foods. There were, of course, exceptions, but primarily we ate real foods made from real ingredients and those ingredients did not include a lengthy list of unrecognizables.

For a number of years I relied heavily on the pre-packaged baking mixes many of us find in the baking aisles at the local grocery store. This allowed me to have things like fresh-baked muffins, cookies, pancakes, and oatmeal on hand for my family. I suppose those are better than pre-made, pre-packaged foods, but they still aren't quite as good as real homemade goods, and over time the cost grew increasingly prohibitive. Prices kept rising as portions kept shrinking, and that makes it hard to maintain a reasonable grocery budget and feed a growing crowd of four kids.

Then I began to go back to more baking from scratch. That gave me great peace of mind in what I was putting into my family's stomachs and the ability to modify and control ingredients if I so chose by mixing up whole-grain foods and using real fat sources that the body could more easily recognize and process (and which were not hydrogenated industrial versions masquerading as the "real thing"—the more I came to learn and understand about traditional foods and fats, the more I came to really dislike the ingredients and modified fats and fillers in commercial foods and baking mixes).

I may have accomplished peace of mind, but I hadn't accomplished adding hours to my day. As a part-time freelance copywriter and part-time small-scale homesteader I had some control over how I spent my time and in choosing to prioritize wholesome food production at home, but there were also things I could not control (like slogging through evening homework sessions with over-burdened elementary school kids...not that I have an opinion on that...). Convenience foods and mixes continued to have great appeal, despite the drawbacks of poor price, portions, value, and ingredients. I wanted and needed the convenience, but I didn't want the cost in any respect.

Basically, as I've seen many others say, despite my best intentions regular scratch cooking and baking for these foods just wasn't happening. I had to go back to the quick mixes or find a better way. I then started coming across a number of "fake it" recipes online that helped me nicely bridge this divide. These were recipes made from staple ingredients I already had in my pantry, which already had a place on my regular grocery list—ingredients I knew, for foods my family loved and that I could feel good about giving them. What resulted was a number of reliable recipes for make-ahead convenience mixes that I began to use steadily.

My practice now has become to take a day every now and again and dedicate that time to stock-piling convenience mixes for everyday use (to estimate say every month or two, depending on how many mixes you make, how much baking and cooking you do, and how often you go through them). Really, this task never takes me an entire day...more like a few hours to measure, mix, and prepare several batches of everything you see here in this book. When I have my "make-ahead" afternoon I basically restock my pantry with all of these staple mixes for the coming month or more.

Having these homemade mixes on hand makes it easy for me to quickly prepare baked goods in the evening for snacks and lunches; fresh muffins, pancakes, or waffles in the morning for a wholesome, filling breakfast; biscuits to go with dinner; and also to have on hand homemade Bisquick® or baking mix (a much cheaper version!). In addition I am able to keep on hand a cheap and easy version of instant oatmeal so I can still send the kids out the door in limited time in the mornings with a hearty breakfast in their bellies. For just about three hours of my time every month or two, I call that an excellent return on my investment.

And so out of this practice and my come-and-go love of organization this book was born. This short but handy reference will make quick work of your day preparing homemade mixes for your family. I'm sure you'll find just as I and many others have that a little time spent in preparation ahead of time will prove invaluable in the long run, and you'll come to really appreciate the time you've invested.

Storing and Labeling Your Mixes

Before jumping right to the recipes, let's talk just a little bit about the best ways to store and label your pre-made mixes.

Home cooks have a number of options available to them in terms of storage for all manner of goods. Some are more suited to long-term and repeat use for dry goods such as these.

Tupperware or Rubbermaid

Tupperware or other storage containers are one idea and you may find these stack and store nicely for you. If you choose a Tupperware-style storage container you'll definitely want to be sure it has a tight-fitting cover that remains air-tight so that humidity or insects do not become a problem. Screw-type lids are probably the safest bet so that they are not popped open as they are bumped and moved around.

Storage Bags

Plastic storage bags are another good option. Many people use Ziploc-style bags for storing pre-made mixes because you can get a lot of them for very cheap money. Again, you'll want to make sure that you choose a good-quality baggie and that any bags you choose will reliably seal well (even if sugar or salt granules creep into the track—I've known this to be an issue, especially when bagging ingredients like salt and brown sugar). Keep in mind also that the seals must hold if stacked on top of each other. They should be heavy enough not to puncture easily, either. You DO NOT want the mess of bursting bags of flour-based mixes all over your kitchen, pantry, or cabinets!

One of the drawbacks to using baggies (in addition to those cautions already mentioned), is that you'll pretty much throw them away after using the mix and you'll need to buy more each time you prepare mixes. It can also be a bit of a battle getting the ingredients into the bags, as they do not stand up on their own. Not only does this have the potential of making a bigger mess than necessary, but you'll also find it takes longer to compile your mixes. You'll end up wasting a lot of unnecessary time.

Best All-Around Option: Mason Jars

For my time and money the absolute best storage solution I've found, one that is both handy and "green" (really the ultimate in earth-friendliness over plastic options), is to use good, old-fashioned glass Mason jars (or any other canning jar of preference). For most batches listed here a one-quart canning jar is just perfect. (The only exceptions would be double-sized batches which require two-quart or half-gallon jars, or perhaps the all-purpose baking mix [Homemade Bisquick®]...although certainly large canning jars are a great storage option for your all-purpose baking mix, too.)

Canning jars offer the advantages of being

   · Airtight
   · Simple to fill very quickly
   · Easy to label
   · Reusable
   · Easy to clean and sterilize
   · Able to take a beating and last a lifetime (believe me—I've dropped enough to know!)
   · Great-looking—you'll be happy to store these homey-looking jars and mixes on an open shelf; your food can become a part of your décor!

Old or second-hand jars are just as good as new as long as they are not cracked. If necessary, simply replace any rusting lids and rings. However, it is certainly worth investing a little in some new jars as well (which will come complete with the lids and rings). It's an expenditure you'll only make once and at approximately $1.00 per jar you will still be saving money even on your first mix day—even filled with a batch of mix the end cost will not equal the $2.50 or more you'd be paying for bagged mixes in the store, and then you'll have the jars already on hand for every subsequent session.

A Fast and Simple Canning Jar Setup

This book has been written with mason jars in mind as the storage option of choice. The setup I use on every mix day is very simple, and in fact everything I needed when I first started making my own mixes were things I already had here at home—including the mix ingredients, since they are all such simple things I was already using. Since I can a lot of foods, I even had all the jars I needed.

My storage and labeling setup from start to finish consists of just these items:

- One- and two-quart Mason jars, regular mouth size*

- A large-mouth canning funnel designed to fit canning jars (found anywhere you buy canning jars—DEFINTELY worth the dollar or two investment to save you time, mess and sanity!! Only a canning funnel has a wide enough bottom opening to allow sugars and flours to flow through without becoming blocked.)

- Printable paper labels for the tops of jars identifying the contents and including mixing and baking instructions**

Other than this all you need are the ingredients to make whatever recipes you like and a set of measuring cups and measuring spoons.

*You will likely use mostly one-quart size jars; for instant oatmeal mixes, all-purpose baking mix, and some mixes that you prefer to have handy in larger double batches you might like to have some two-quart jars on hand. Two-quart jars are a bit harder to come by and may be limited in availability through brick-and-mortar retailers, but they are easy to find through online retailers like Amazon and others. Currently they run around $13 for 6 jars with lids.

**Copy-ready paper labels are included at the end of this book and are also available in larger sheets available in a completely printable Make-Ahead Mix Day Companion PDF, available for 99 cents at my website, www.TheHomemadeHomestead.com. The Companion PDF includes all of the recipes and preparation lists found here in this book and also includes 21 different sheets of four or six labels, one sheet for each recipe, with the name of the mix and complete baking instructions. Labels in the PDF are color-coded to match the recipe they belong to in order to make it that much faster for you to combine, cover, and label your mixes. With either the PDF labels or the copy-ready versions here all you need to do is print the pages you need, cut the labels out, and place the paper label on top of the lid and under the ring to secure. There is no gluing, adhesive, special paper or expensive pre-fab label paper to buy; the printable labels require only normal printer paper.

Some Thoughts on Ingredient Selection

I won't delve deeply into what the best ingredients are for you to use; that is a personal choice based on preference, dietary, and probably to an extent ethical considerations, too. No one but you can decide what is best to put into your food. There are, however, a couple of points worth touching upon in the interest of shelf-life and flexibility to suit certain dietary preferences.

Recipe Flexibility and Substitution

There is some amount of flexibility in these recipes, limited primarily to ingredient exchange or substitution. You should have no troubles using these recipes with whatever related ingredients or substitutions you would normally use in your everyday baking and cooking, so therefore you should easily be able to adjust these recipes to suit your dietary needs or preferences. The exception that you might find is that where volume and measurements are different for the products you use, you may need to adjust the quantities of liquids and/or fats used when preparing the mix.

Mostly I am speaking to the desire to exchange different types of flour in and out of these recipes. I expect these recipes will work as well with whatever flours you normally use for similar baking items. All-purpose white flour is what is called for in each of these recipes, but a whole-grain white flour or other substitution should perform adequately, too. Likewise, a specialty flour that you might use in the case of an allergy or gluten intolerance, such as a rice flour, should also work in the mixes (however if there is a normal adjustment or recipe modification you typically employ in other recipes, you might want to try that here). I would suggest that if you are using significantly different ingredients you try the recipe out with a practice batch before bottling up a whole pantry's worth of pre-made mixes.

The recipe for the All-Purpose Baking Mix (homemade Bisquick®) is especially flexible in terms of flours used. If you are aiming to get more whole grains in your household diet try using half all-purpose flour and half whole-wheat flour, or all whole-grain white flour. You might try substituting oat flour

15

or something similar for part or all of the white flour as well. You may find some minor difference in texture or density but it should be negligible and certainly palatable, and should be no more different than you would normally expect from baking with these sorts of products (after all, we do need to accept some difference in any end product made with different ingredients).

Note that if the quantity exchange is different, you may need to adjust the liquid or fat (lard, shortening, butter or oil) when preparing the mixes (you may also find some additional liquid adjustment necessary the more whole-grain products you use). For example, if a mix calls for ½ cup white sugar and you use a sugar substitute that substitutes in at a lower amount, say ¼ cup as an example, you may have to reduce the amount of oil or butter used to prepare the mix so that it is not too runny. This will vary by mix and product. However products that substitute at the same volume as what is called for in the original recipe should work well enough without need for real modification. For instance, if you are simply changing out a cup of white all-purpose flour for a cup of white whole wheat flour or a cup of rice flour in order to have a gluten-free product, you probably will not need to make any other adjustment to achieve a desirable end-product (unless specifically stated on the product). Do note, however, that rice flour normally absorbs more water and so you may need to add a bit of water to achieve normal batter consistency when using rice flour as a substitute.

Finally, it is worth mentioning that you also have some flexibility in preparing the mixes when you bake or cook them as well. Most of the mixes in this book call for eggs; if you normally use an egg substitute or something else, use that same substitution and ratio for preparing these mixes. They also call primarily for butter, but an equal measurement of your preferred baking or cooking oil will also work, although you may find you need to add a tablespoon or two of water as well. (Although I prefer and generally bake with butter, being a homesteader with a Jersey cow and a fresh supply and also a believer in eating more traditional foods that I believe the body is better able to recognize and process, I've made these recipes with both butter and oil. There is a slight difference in consistency and spreading in things like the cookies, but again, it's negligible and will not result in a disappointing baked good. You should certainly use whatever works best for you, or whatever you believe to be the best for you and yours.)

Shelf Life and Fat Selection

On that note, let's take just a minute to talk about the fats used in the mixes themselves.

As mentioned, my family and home is something of a little homestead. We produce much of what we eat and raise animals for dairy and meat. I try very hard to utilize as much of what we produce here as possible and so I frequently use fats that other people don't usually use to the same extent I do. Both from the consideration of price and budgeting and also from the perspective of what is available to me, I tend to use more animal-based, basic fats, even in my mixes. Of course there is a range of availability and affordability, as well as convenience, preference, and other considerations out there that will impact what you choose to use in terms of the fats you bake with or make your mixes with.

I am by no means trying to preach one source over another; that is up to you to decide. I am simply sharing my choice and process. The reason I really mention this is that the choice of the fats you use in certain of these recipes might affect their shelf life and stability. The fat you bake with when you prepare a dry mix doesn't make all that much difference, and none in terms of shelf life, but it can potentially make a difference in the stability of the all-purpose baking mix listed in this book.

What you basically need to know is this: vegetable shortenings, Crisco®, and lard that you buy in the typical grocery store on the shelf in the baking aisle are all shelf-stable products. If you use one of these products you can store the mix as you would store a box of Bisquick®, Jiffy® Mix, biscuit mix, etc. Any cool, dry place where you keep dry goods safely should be just as good for the mix you create. (For your protection and mine, though, please see the disclaimer*** at the end of this book.)

The difference comes in if you are using real, natural products like true lard. Vegetable shortenings and store-bought lard are shelf-stable because they are hydrogenated. Store lard starts out as the same product as real lard (rendered pork fat), but is then put through the hydrogenation process to make it able to sit and store at room temperature, almost indefinitely. Real lard (that which you buy or render yourself which has not been hydrogenated), is not truly stable at room temperature. It is not all that fragile, but it does require refrigeration or freezing for longer life and safety. I do normally use real lard when I prepare my homemade Bisquick because I am making a concerted effort to decrease or eliminate hydrogenated foods in our household diet, just for the health of it. I simply refrigerate my container of mix to store it once it is prepared and between uses. Other than that there is no difference. If you want to keep it longer, or if space considerations make it a better option for you, this mix freezes and preserves well, also, and again there is no performance difference.

The bottom line is that a shelf-stable fat source should make a shelf-stable mix that can be stored at room temperature, but if your fat source is otherwise handled then you should handle and store the end mix as you would the fat itself.***

How Much Does It Take?

The only other question left, then, a question I am often asked when someone wants to start making their own homemade baking mixes, is, "How much do I need?" In other words, how much of each ingredient should you buy and have on hand for your make-ahead mix day?

Well of course there is not one simple answer to this question. If there were it would be, "It depends how many mixes you plan to make." That is also the obvious answer, so let's see if we can come up with some idea.

In order to give you that idea, let me give you an estimate of the ingredients I used on my last "Mix Day" and how many mixes I made from that list. Before I do, though, you should note that I bake probably at least four out of seven nights per week, sometimes more, to supplement in lunches and that I also like to "go big" when I set aside an afternoon to do something like stock my pantry with quick-mix baking mixes. I usually figure I should maximize the time I set aside to do things like this and make it last so that I do not have to repeat it in a week or two, and so that the task doesn't become a practice in tedium. (On average an afternoon of mixing probably will last me around 6 weeks...unless we're particularly hungry or stricken with a sweet tooth.)

Moving on to particulars, this is the list of groceries I used on my last Mix Day:

- 25 Lbs. flour
- 10 Lbs. white sugar
- 5 Lbs. brown sugar
- 4 ½ Lbs. Oats
- 1 eight-ounce can baking powder
- 1 eight-ounce can baking cocoa
- 1 24-ounce bag chocolate chips
- 2 cups lard (shortening)
- 1 jar (32 ounces) peanut butter
- Baking soda (about ¼ to ½ cup)
- Salt (about ¼ to ½ cup)

Out of this I made (in just about two and a half to three hours):

- 2 Gallons Homemade Bisquick®/All-Purpose Baking Mix

18

· 1 ½ Gallons Instant Oatmeal
· 4 quarts Muffin Mix
· 20 Quarts Cookie Mix
· 2 Quarts Cake Mix
· 4 Quarts Brownie Mix

Put another way, that translates into 30 batches of mixes for baked goods (cookies, brownies, cakes, etc.), plus a large (8 quarts) all-around versatile baking mix, plus a large (6 quarts) batch of easy instant oatmeal mix for the mornings (divided into 2 flavors). (And then of course I didn't use every last drop of every single thing, so there is a little of this and that left over for other uses). (Note the average batch size for cookies in this book is two dozen, the average muffin recipe makes one dozen, and cake and brownie mixes make one 9 x 13 pan each.)

Realizing this is something of a vague answer, hopefully you can use it to give you some idea of how much you need for the quantity you want to make; or, you could just make as much as I did and let it last you a long while like I do. The shelf life on these mixes under typical good household storage conditions is quite long—months, assuming your family lets them last that long—so there's really nothing to lose from "over" preparing your pantry.

A Couple Noteworthy Ideas

Almost as a side note, it's worth taking a minute to mention a couple of other ideas and uses for the mixes in this book. Two really come to mind: the potential for gift-giving and the potential as fundraisers (and possible money-makers depending on your situation, where you live, and local ordinances that would govern something like this in your locale).

These mixes—the cookie, brownie, and muffin mixes in particular—have proven to be great fundraisers for various groups my children have been involved with. They require just the minimum of ingredients (as discussed) and of course the jars and labels, and then just an investment of volunteer time to make the mixes (we found this went really quickly with an assembly line of helpers, and we were able to prepare about four-dozen mixes in an hour). We were able to roughly double our investment in ingredients and materials. If you have a good base of people willing to donate ingredients (perhaps assigning one item per family or donor) and a box or two of jars, you could reasonably make the mixes for little or no money and see a 500% profit (or more or less, depending on where you choose to price them).

You probably do not even need me to tell you anything about the gift-giving potential of these mixes; we've probably all received something similar from time to time (and I know having these on hand has pulled me out of a jam on more than one occasion with an unexpected holiday guest or last-minute gift need! Housewarmings, anyone?). Yes, homemade jar mixes are excellent useful, appreciated gifts.

Starting with these basic jar mixes, simply dress up the jars with a round of fabric or even an upside-down decorative muffin paper under the identification/instruction label, and then maybe add some ribbon or raffia, twine, etc. If you want to build your gift a little more make a gift basket out of it with a nice mixing bowl, a set of measuring cups or spoons, wooden spoons, and so on. The options are too many to list so have fun with it, but both of these ideas are something else to keep in mind or hold onto for the future when some bright idea is called for!

About This Book's Organization

We've finally now dispensed with most of the preliminary discussions, and we're very nearly ready to move on to the good stuff—the recipes!

From here on out this book is very simple; just the recipes, for the most part. As you go through them you'll note that each "page" from here to the end of the recipes is very brief. This has been very intentionally done, so as to make it easier for you when you actually sit down to compile your mixes.

The thought when writing this book was that when you sit down, ingredients and jars gathered, ready to work, you need something that is very easy to follow; and so that is how the recipes and pages were arranged—each to its own page, nothing else there to distract or make it difficult to follow the directions for the mix at hand.

The result of this has been that some of the recipes are very similar; in some cases the same, in fact, only figured to make a larger batch. I have selected out a few of the recipes that I and others like to have on hand in larger batches and listed them as both a one-quart batch and then separately as a two-quart "double batch" recipe. You simply have to tap or turn through to the batch/recipe that suits your need and follow down the list of ingredients and measurements.

Following each recipe I have also listed the instructions for preparing and baking the mix when the time comes. I did, of course, want to provide you with all of the information needed to enjoy these recipes, even though you won't necessarily bake the mix on the day you prepare it. In the Printable Companion PDF available on my website, this is done a little differently—on the recipe pages you get only the recipe and the preparation instructions are saved for the label, where they are really needed. This makes it just that much faster on mix day, and that much easier on the day you want to bake a given mix (no need to come back here to find the right set of instructions for the right mix—having the labels on the jar is a real time-saver, too!).

And now finally, it is time to get to the recipes. Take a look and see what strikes you, grab your baking staples, and do, above all, **Enjoy**!

Brownies

To each **1 quart** jar add:

(batch makes one 9x13 pan)

- · 2 cups sugar
- · 1 cup flour
- · ⅔ cup cocoa
- · ½ teaspoon salt
- · ½ teaspoon baking powder

To prepare add:

- · 4 eggs
- · 1 cup vegetable oil
- · 2 teaspoons vanilla

Bake at 350° in greased pan for 23 minutes or until done

Chocolate Chip Cookies

To each **1 quart** jar add:

· 1 cup flour

· ½ cup brown sugar

· ¼ cup white sugar

· ½ teaspoon baking soda

· ½ teaspoon salt

· ¾ cup chocolate chips

To prepare add:

· 1 stick softened butter (½ cup)

· 1 egg

· ½ teaspoon vanilla

Bake at 350° for 9 to 11 minutes or until done

Double Batch Chocolate Chip Cookie Mix

To each 1 quart jar add:

- · 2 cups flour
- · 1 cup brown sugar
- · ½ cup white sugar
- · 1 teaspoon baking soda
- · 1 teaspoon salt
- · 1 ½ cups chocolate chips

To prepare add:

- · 2 sticks softened butter (1 cup)
- · 2 eggs
- · 1 teaspoon vanilla

Bake at 350° for 9 to 11 minutes or until done

Sugar Cookies

To each 1 quart jar add:

- · 1 ½ cups flour
- · ¾ cup white sugar
- · ½ teaspoon baking powder
- · ½ teaspoon baking soda
- · ½ teaspoon salt

To prepare add:

- · 1 stick softened butter (½ cup)
- · 1 egg
- · ½ teaspoon vanilla

Bake at 350° for 9 to 11 minutes or until done

Double Batch Sugar Cookie Mix

To each 2 quart jar add:

- · 3 cups flour
- · 1 ½ cups white sugar
- · 1 teaspoon baking powder
- · 1 teaspoon baking soda
- · 1 teaspoon salt

To prepare add:

- · 2 sticks softened butter (1 cup)
- · 2 eggs
- · 1 teaspoon vanilla

Bake at 350° for 9 to 11 minutes or until done

Oatmeal Cookies

To each 1 Quart jar add:

- · 1 cup flour
- · ½ cup white sugar
- · ½ cup brown sugar
- · 1 ½ cup rolled oats
- · ½ teaspoon baking soda
- · ½ teaspoon salt
- · 1 teaspoon cinnamon

To prepare add:

- · 1 stick melted butter (½ cup)
- · 1 egg
- · ½ teaspoon vanilla

Bake at 350° for 9 to 11 minutes or until done

Oatmeal Chocolate Chip Cookies

To each 1 Quart jar add:

- · 1 cup flour
- · ½ cup white sugar
- · ½ cup brown sugar
- · 1 ½ cup rolled oats
- · ½ teaspoon baking soda
- · ½ teaspoon salt
- · 1 teaspoon cinnamon
- · ½ cup chocolate chips

To prepare add:

- · 1 stick melted butter (½ cup)
- · 1 egg
- · ½ teaspoon vanilla

Bake at 350° for 9 to 11 minutes or until done

Gingerbread Cookies

To each 1 quart jar add:

- · 1 ¾ cups flour
- · ¾ cup brown sugar
- · ¾ teaspoon baking soda
- · ½ teaspoon salt
- · 1 ½ teaspoons ginger
- · 1 ½ teaspoons cinnamon
- · ¼ teaspoon nutmeg
- · ¼ teaspoon cloves

To prepare add:

- · 1 stick softened butter (½ cup)
- · 1 egg
- · ⅛ cup molasses

Roll into balls or drop and sprinkle with sugar
Bake at 350° for 9 to 11 minutes or until done

Double Batch Gingerbread Cookies

To each 2 quart jar add:

- · 3 ½ cups flour
- · 1 ½ cups brown sugar
- · 1 ½ teaspoons baking soda
- · 1 teaspoon salt
- · 1 tablespoon ginger
- · 1 tablespoon cinnamon
- · ½ teaspoon nutmeg
- · ½ teaspoon cloves

To prepare add:

- · 2 sticks softened butter (1 cup)
- · 2 eggs
- · ¼ cup molasses

Roll into balls or drop and sprinkle with sugar

Bake at 350° for 9 to 11 minutes or until done

Peanut Butter Cookies

To make 4, 1-quart jar mixes:

Step 1: In a mixing bowl combine 6 cups flour and 2 cups peanut butter. Mix to combine and crumble mixture with fingers until the mix resembles coarse crumbs.

Step 2: To each 1 quart jar add:

- · 2 cups peanut butter and flour mixture
- · ¾ cup sugar
- · ½ teaspoon baking powder
- · ½ teaspoon baking soda
- · ½ teaspoon salt

To prepare add:

- · 1 stick softened cup butter (½ cup)
- · 1 egg
- · ½ teaspoon vanilla

Roll into balls and flatten or drop; sprinkle with sugar if desired

Bake at 350° for 9 to 11 minutes or until done

Chocolate Cake Mix

To each 1 quart jar add:

- · 2 cups flour
- · 1 ½ cups sugar
- · 1 tablespoon baking powder
- · ½ cup cocoa powder

To prepare add:

- · ¾ cup milk
- · 1 stick butter (½ cup)
- · 3 eggs
- · 1 teaspoon vanilla

Beat with mixer for 2 minutes

Pour into greased and floured 9 x 13 pan*

Bake at 350° for 35 minutes or until done

*May also be baked in 2 round or square pans, or in cupcake tins but reduce baking time: cupcakes 13-15 min; small pans 20 min.

White Cake Mix

To each 1 quart jar add:

- · 2 cups flour
- · 1 ½ cup sugar
- · 1 tablespoon baking powder

To prepare add:

- · ¾ cup milk
- · 1 stick butter (½ cup)
- · 3 eggs
- · 1 teaspoon vanilla

Beat with mixer for 2 minutes

Pour into greased and floured 9 x 13 pan*

Bake at 350° for 35 minutes or until done

*May also be baked in 2 round or square pans, or in cupcake tins   but reduce baking time: cupcakes 13-15 min; small pans 20 min.

Plain Muffin Mix

To each 1 quart jar add:

      · 2 cups all-purpose flour

      · ¾ cup sugar

      · 2 ¼ teaspoons baking powder

      · ½ teaspoon salt

To prepare add:

      · 1 stick melted butter (½ cup)

      · 1 egg

      · 1 cup milk

*If desired, may add ½ cup additions (nuts, berries, dried fruit)

*May also top with cinnamon sugar if desired

Grease or line muffin cups

Fill ⅔ full with batter

Bake at 400° for 18 to 20 minutes or until done

Chocolate Chip Muffin Mix

To each 1 quart jar add:

>· 2 cups all-purpose flour
>
>· ¾ cup sugar
>
>· 2 ¼ teaspoons baking powder
>
>· ½ teaspoon salt
>
>· ½ cup chocolate chips

To prepare add:

>· 1 stick melted butter (½ cup)
>
>· 1 egg
>
>· 1 cup milk

Grease or line muffin cups

Fill ⅔ full with batter

Bake at 400° for 18 to 20 minutes or until done

Spiced Muffin Mix

To each 1 quart jar add:

- · 2 cups all-purpose flour
- · ¾ cup sugar
- · 2 ¼ teaspoons baking powder
- · ½ teaspoon salt
- · ½ teaspoon cinnamon
- · ½ teaspoon nutmeg

To prepare add:

- · 1 stick melted butter (½ cup)
- · 1 egg
- · 1 cup milk

Grease or line muffin cups

Fill ⅔ full with batter

Bake at 400° for 18 to 20 minutes or until done

Cappuccino Muffin Mix

To each 1 quart jar add:

- · 2 cups all-purpose flour
- · ¾ cup sugar
- · 2 ¼ teaspoons baking powder
- · ½ teaspoon salt
- · ½ cup semi-sweet chocolate chips
- · ½ teaspoon instant coffee
- · ½ teaspoon cinnamon (optional)
- · ½ teaspoon nutmeg (optional)

To prepare add:

- · 1 stick melted butter (½ cup)
- · 1 egg
- · 1 cup milk

Grease or line muffin cups

Fill ⅔ full with batter

Bake at 400° for 18 to 20 minutes or until done

All-Purpose Baking Mix (Bisquick Style)

Step 1: In a mixing bowl combine and mix through:

· 20 cups all-purpose flour (equal to one 5 lb. bag)

· 3 tablespoons salt

· 7 tablespoons sugar

· ⅔ cup baking powder

Step 2: Using a pastry cutter or clean hands and fingers, cut in:

· 2 cups lard or vegetable shortening

Mix/cut until pea-sized crumbs are distributed throughout

Store in air-tight container (large Rubbermaid or mason jars)

Makes about 2 gallons

To prepare:

Use as you would in any Bisquick, baking mix, or biscuit mix recipe

Use in equal amounts as called for in recipe

Quick Morning Pancake Mix

To each 1 quart jar add:

    · 2 cups prepared homemade All-Purpose Baking mix

    To prepare add:

    · 1 cup milk

    · 2 eggs

Cook on griddle or flat-bottomed pan over medium heat

Plain Unsweetened Instant Oatmeal Mix

Step 1: In a large bowl combine and mix through:

· 7 cups quick oats

· 2 teaspoons salt

Step 2: Using a blender or a food processor, blend 3 cups quick oats until powdery. Add to oat and salt mixture and stir well to combine. Store in 2-quart mason jars.

To prepare:

· Combine ½ cup oatmeal mix and ¾ cup boiling water in bowl.

· Stir to combine and let sit for 1 minute, then eat.

· Can add honey, maple syrup, berries, cream, or other flavorings.

Microwave directions:

· Combine ½ cup oatmeal mix and ¾ cup water in bowl.

· Stir to combine and microwave on high for 1 minute.

· Let sit 1 minute to thicken before eating.

Plain Sweetened Instant Oatmeal Mix

Step 1: In a large bowl combine and mix through:

- · 7 cups quick oats
- · 2 cups white sugar
- · 2 teaspoons salt

· *May add dried fruit or other additions as desired.

Step 2: Using a blender or a food processor, blend 3 cups quick oats until powdery. Add to oat mixture and stir well to combine. Store in 2-quart mason jars.

To prepare:

· Combine ½ cup oatmeal mix and ¾ cup boiling water in bowl.

· Stir to combine and let sit for 1 minute before eating.

· Can add preferred flavorings as desired.

Microwave directions:

· Combine ½ cup oatmeal mix and ¾ cup water in bowl.

· Stir to combine and microwave on high for 1 minute.

· Let sit 1 minute to thicken before eating.

Brown Sugar & Cinnamon Instant Oatmeal Mix

Step 1: In a large bowl combine and mix through:

· 7 cups quick oats

· 1 cup white sugar

· 1 cup brown sugar

· 2 teaspoons salt

· 4 teaspoons cinnamon

Step 2: Using a blender or a food processor, blend 3 cups quick oats until powdery. Add to oat mixture and stir well to combine. Store in 2-quart mason jars.

To prepare:

· Combine ½ cup oatmeal mix and ¾ cup boiling water in bowl.

· Stir to combine and let sit for 1 minute before eating.

Microwave directions:

· Combine ½ cup oatmeal mix and ¾ cup water in bowl.

· Stir to combine and microwave on high for 1 minute.

· Let sit 1 minute to thicken before eating.

Making Fast Work of Your Mix Day

If you head into your make-ahead mix day prepared, you'll make fast work of the task and the few hours will fly by. Before you know it you'll have a fully-stocked pantry that you can be proud of.

The trick to making fast work of the day is to gather all of your ingredients ahead of time, making sure you have plenty of staples so that you aren't faced with having to make any runs out to the store. This includes having your mason jars or storage containers of choice on-hand in adequate numbers as well. If you choose take advantage of the copy-ready container labels in this book, or perhaps the printer-ready formats in the companion PDF, you'll make your time in the kitchen move along smoothly if you have your selected labels trimmed and ready before you begin mixing.

It's all intended to make short work of saving time and money while feeling good about the treats and convenience foods you provide for you and yours—making your life easier even as you work harder to provide good foods you can believe in!

Appendix: Copy-Ready Mix Labels

The following pages contain labels for the tops of the jar mixes after they have been prepared. They have been sized to fit between the two-piece lids that come with the canning jars, for either one-quart or two-quart jars. To use, simply make enough photocopies of the labels you need, cut, and then place the appropriate label on top of the first jar lid and secure with the screw ring.

Due to space constraints in this print version you will find only two labels per page. However, the downloadable Make-Ahead Mix Day Printable Companion remains available for 99 cents via the "Make-Ahead Mix Day" link at www.thehomemadehomestead.com. In the printable companion you will find four or six labels (in color) per standard page (depending on jar size) that you can simply print directly from your computer without the need to photocopy. Many find this to be a simpler alternative, although the choice is certainly yours. Whatever you decide, I hope you find these labels useful and time-saving!

Brownie Label

Brownies
Add:
4 eggs
1 cup melted butter or
vegetable oil
2 TSP vanilla extract
Bake in greased pan at
350° for 23 minutes

Brownies
Add:
4 eggs
1 cup melted butter or
vegetable oil
2 TSP vanilla extract
Bake in greased pan at
350° for 23 minutes

Chocolate Chip Cookie Label

Chocolate Chip Cookies
Add:
½ C soft butter
1 egg
½ TSP vanilla extract
Bake at 350° for 9-11 mins.

Chocolate Chip Cookies
Add:
½ C soft butter
1 egg
½ TSP vanilla extract
Bake at 350° for 9-11 mins.

Double Batch Chocolate Chip Cookie Label

Double Batch Chocolate Chip Cookies
Add:
2 sticks soft butter (1 cup)
2 eggs
1 TSP vanilla extract
Bake at 350° for 9-11 minutes

Double Batch Chocolate Chip Cookies
Add:
2 sticks soft butter (1 cup)
2 eggs
1 TSP vanilla extract
Bake at 350° for 9-11 minutes

Sugar Cookie Labels

Sugar Cookies
Add:
1 stick softened butter
1 egg
½ TSP vanilla extract
Roll or drop and bake
at 350° for 9-11
minutes

Sugar Cookies
Add:
1 stick softened butter
1 egg
½ TSP vanilla extract
Roll or drop and bake
at 350° for 9-11
minutes

Double Batch Sugar Cookie Labels

Double Batch Sugar Cookies
Add:
2 sticks softened butter
2 eggs
1 TSP vanilla extract
Roll or drop and bake at 350°
for 9-11 minutes

Double Batch Sugar Cookies
Add:
2 sticks softened butter
2 eggs
1 TSP vanilla extract
Roll or drop and bake at 350°
for 9-11 minutes

Oatmeal Cookie Labels

Oatmeal Cookies
Add:
½ C melted butter
1 egg
½ TSP vanilla extract
Bake at 350° for 9-11
mins.

Oatmeal Cookies
Add:
½ C melted butter
1 egg
½ TSP vanilla extract
Bake at 350° for 9-11
mins.

Oatmeal Chocolate Chip Cookie Labels

Oatmeal Chocolate
Chip Cookies
Add:
½ C melted butter
1 egg
½ TSP vanilla extract
Bake: 350°;9-11 min.

Oatmeal Chocolate
Chip Cookies
Add:
½ C melted butter
1 egg
½ TSP vanilla extract
Bake: 350°;9-11 min.

Gingerbread Cookie Labels

Gingerbread Cookies
½ C soft butter
1 egg
1/8 C molasses
Roll or drop, sprinkle
with sugar
Bake: 350°;9-11 min.

Gingerbread Cookies
½ C soft butter
1 egg
1/8 C molasses
Roll or drop, sprinkle
with sugar
Bake: 350°;9-11 min.

Double Batch Gingerbread Cookie Labels

Double Batch
Gingerbread Cookies
Add:
2 sticks soft butter (1 cup)
2 eggs
1/4 C molasses
Roll or drop and sprinkle with
sugar
Bake at 350° for 9-11 minutes

Double Batch
Gingerbread Cookies
Add:
2 sticks soft butter (1 cup)
2 eggs
1/4 C molasses
Roll or drop and sprinkle with
sugar
Bake at 350° for 9-11 minutes

Peanut Butter Cookie Labels

Peanut Butter Cookies
½ C soft butter
1 egg
½ TSP vanilla
Roll or drop & flatten,
sprinkle with sugar
Bake: 350°;9-11 min.

Peanut Butter Cookies
½ C soft butter
1 egg
½ TSP vanilla
Roll or drop & flatten,
sprinkle with sugar
Bake: 350°;9-11 min.

Chocolate Cake Mix Labels

Chocolate Cake
3/4 C milk
1/2 C soft butter
3 eggs
1 TSP vanilla
Beat with mixer 2 min
Grease, flour 9x13 pan
Bake: 350° for 35 min.

Chocolate Cake
3/4 C milk
1/2 C soft butter
3 eggs
1 TSP vanilla
Beat with mixer 2 min
Grease, flour 9x13 pan
Bake: 350° for 35 min.

White Cake Mix Labels

White Cake
3/4 C milk
1/2 C soft butter
3 eggs
1 TSP vanilla
Beat with mixer 2 min
Grease, flour 9x13 pan
Bake: 350° for 35 min.

White Cake
3/4 C milk
1/2 C soft butter
3 eggs
1 TSP vanilla
Beat with mixer 2 min
Grease, flour 9x13 pan
Bake: 350° for 35 min.

Plain Muffin Mix Labels

Plain Muffins
1/2 C melted butter
1 egg
1 C milk
Top or add additions
(1/2 C) as desired
Line or grease tins,
bake @ 400, 18 min.

Plain Muffins
1/2 C melted butter
1 egg
1 C milk
Top or add additions
(1/2 C) as desired
Line or grease tins,
bake @ 400, 18 min.

Chocolate Chip Muffin Mix Labels

Chocolate Chip
Muffins
1/2 C melted butter
1 egg
1 C milk
Line or grease tins
Bake @ 400, 18 min.

Chocolate Chip
Muffins
1/2 C melted butter
1 egg
1 C milk
Line or grease tins
Bake @ 400, 18 min.

Spiced Muffin Mix Labels

Spiced Muffins
1/2 C melted butter
1 egg
1 C milk
Line or grease tins
Bake @ 400, 18 min.

Spiced Muffins
1/2 C melted butter
1 egg
1 C milk
Line or grease tins
Bake @ 400, 18 min.

Cappuccino Muffin Mix Labels

Cappuccino
Muffins
1/2 C melted butter
1 egg
1 C milk
Line or grease tins
Bake @ 400, 18 min.

Cappuccino
Muffins
1/2 C melted butter
1 egg
1 C milk
Line or grease tins
Bake @ 400, 18 min.

All-Purpose Baking Mix Labels

All Purpose Baking Mix
(Bisquick® Style)

Use as you would use baking
mix in any Bisquick, baking
mix, or biscuit mix recipe

Use in equal amounts as called
for in recipe

All Purpose Baking Mix
(Bisquick® Style)

Use as you would use baking
mix in any Bisquick, baking
mix, or biscuit mix recipe

Use in equal amounts as called
for in recipe

Quick Morning Pancake Mix Labels

Quick Morning
Pancakes
Add:
1 C milk
2 eggs
Cook over medium
heat

Quick Morning
Pancakes
Add:
1 C milk
2 eggs
Cook over medium
heat

Plain Unsweetened Instant Oatmeal Labels

Plain Unsweetened Instant Oatmeal

Combine 1/2 C oatmeal with
3/4 C boiling water
Let sit 1 minute before eating
Can add maple syrup, honey,
berries, cream, or other favorite
flavorings
Microwave directions: Combine
1/2 C oatmeal and 3/4 C water;
cook 1 minute on high

Plain Unsweetened Instant Oatmeal

Combine 1/2 C oatmeal with
3/4 C boiling water
Let sit 1 minute before eating
Can add maple syrup, honey,
berries, cream, or other favorite
flavorings
Microwave directions: Combine
1/2 C oatmeal and 3/4 C water;
cook 1 minute on high

Plain Sweetened Instant Oatmeal Labels

Plain Sweetened Instant Oatmeal

Combine 1/2 C oatmeal with 3/4 C boiling water
Let sit 1 minute before eating
Can add dried fruit, nuts, or other preferred flavorings as desired
Microwave directions: Combine 1/2 C oatmeal and 3/4 C water; cook 1 minute on high

Plain Sweetened Instant Oatmeal

Combine 1/2 C oatmeal with 3/4 C boiling water
Let sit 1 minute before eating
Can add dried fruit, nuts, or other preferred flavorings as desired
Microwave directions: Combine 1/2 C oatmeal and 3/4 C water; cook 1 minute on high

Brown Sugar & Cinnamon Instant Oatmeal Labels

Brown Sugar & Cinnamon Instant Oatmeal

Combine 1/2 C oatmeal with
3/4 C boiling water
Let sit 1 minute before eating
Microwave directions: Combine
1/2 C oatmeal and 3/4 C water;
cook 1 minute on high

Brown Sugar & Cinnamon Instant Oatmeal

Combine 1/2 C oatmeal with
3/4 C boiling water
Let sit 1 minute before eating
Microwave directions: Combine
1/2 C oatmeal and 3/4 C water;
cook 1 minute on high

About the Author

Homesteading, house-holding, farming, gardening, being a wife and mother, and yes writing, too, represent the majority of ways Mary Ellen Ward spends her days. Believing in living well and eating well and days that end in a feeling of accomplishment, these things that seem much too much like "work" to others are the things she truly enjoys, and the ways she chooses to spend her days. She considers herself highly fortunate to be able to do so, and enjoys sharing her knowledge and experiences with others with similar inclinations. Look for more titles to come from Mary in the near future.

Credits & Resources

Brought to you by Mary Ellen Ward

And

www.thehomemadehomestead.com

Some recipes in this book are the creation of Mary Ellen Ward. Others are either sourced, inspired, or modified from recipes published by the following websites:

www.fakeitfrugal.blogspot.com

www.tasteofhome.com

www.coffeebreakwithlizandkate.com

www.afewshortcuts.com

Please visit these very useful websites!

Credit for all photos and images inside this book goes to the talented Miss Emily R. Putney.

More to Come from This Author

There are more titles and helpful resources to come from this author in the near future, including homesteading titles and also more tips and resources to help you meet the challenges of keeping a budget, house, and home while eating well and providing for your family. Please join in and subscribe to The Homemade Homestead at www.thehomemadehomestead.com to stay updated as more titles of interest are published.

Alternatively, if you prefer not to follow along with site updates you can also eMail the author at The Homemade Homestead and ask to be included only in emails pertaining to new publications. A Contact link is available on-site. Please rest assured that your contact will be used ONLY for updates from this author and her website, and will NEVER be sold to a third party without your permission!

And finally, before you go, a generous ...

Thank You

...for reading this book!

~If you have enjoyed this book and/or found any small part of it useful, your honest review will be very much appreciated by both the author and fellow and future readers. Thoughtful reviews help good books to be found!~

Made in the USA
Middletown, DE
10 January 2024

47608407R00042